EXTREME SURVIVAL IN THE MILITARY

SURVIVING CAPTIVITY

EXTREME SURVIVAL IN THE MILITARY

EXTREME SURVIVAL IN THE MILITARY

SURVIVING CAPTIVITY

CHRIS McNAB

Introduction by Colonel John T. Carney. Jr., USAF-Ret.
President, Special Operations Warrior Foundation

MASON CREST

Mason Crest
450 Parkway Drive, Suite D
Broomall, PA 19008
www.masoncrest.com

Printed and bound in the United States of America.

10 9 8 7 6 5 4 3 2 1

Series ISBN: 978-1-4222-3081-7
ISBN: 978-1-4222-3089-3
ebook ISBN: 978-1-4222-8781-1

Cataloging-in-Publication Data on file with the Library of Congress.

Picture Credits
Corbis: 11, 14, 22, 26, 28, 34, 36, 38, 42; **TRH:** 8, 10, 12, 13, 18, 20, 44, 47, 53, 54
Illustrations courtesy of De Agostini UK and the following supplied by Patrick Mulrey: 21, 24, 30, 31, 32, 33, 37, 41, 48, 55

ACKNOWLEDGMENT
For authenticating this book, the Publishers would like to thank the Public Affairs Offices of the U.S. Special Operations Command, MacDill AFB, FL.; Army Special Operations Command, Fort Bragg, N.C.; Navy Special Warfare Command, Coronado, CA.; and the Air Force Special Operations Command, Hurlbert Field, FL.

IMPORTANT NOTICE
The survival techniques and information described in this publication are for educational use only. The publisher is not responsible for any direct, indirect, incidental or consequential damages as a result of the uses or misuses of the techniques and information within.

DEDICATION
This book is dedicated to those who perished in the terrorist attacks of September 11, 2001, and to the Special Forces soldiers who continually serve to defend freedom.

CONTENTS

KEY ICONS TO LOOK FOR:

Text-Dependent Questions: These questions send the reader back to the text for more careful attention to the evidence presented there.

Words to Understand: These words with their easy-to-understand definitions will increase the reader's understanding of the text, while building vocabulary skills.

Series Glossary of Key Terms: This back-of-the book glossary contains terminology used throughout this series. Words found here increase the reader's ability to read and comprehend higher-level books and articles in this field.

Research Projects: Readers are pointed toward areas of further inquiry connected to each chapter. Suggestions are provided for projects that encourage deeper research and analysis.

Sidebars: This boxed material within the main text allows readers to build knowledge, gain insights, explore possibilities, and broaden their perspectives by weaving together additional information to provide realistic and holistic perspectives.

INTRODUCTION

Elite forces are the tip of Freedom's spear. These small, special units are universally the first to engage, whether on reconnaissance missions into denied territory for larger, conventional forces or in direct action, surgical operations, preemptive strikes, retaliatory action, and hostage rescues. They lead the way in today's war on terrorism, the war on drugs, the war on transnational unrest, and in humanitarian operations as well as nation building. When large scale warfare erupts, they offer theater commanders a wide variety of unique, unconventional options.

Most such units are regionally oriented, acclimated to the culture and conversant in the languages of the areas where they operate. Since they deploy to those areas regularly, often for combined training exercises with indigenous forces, these elite units also serve as peacetime "global scouts" and "diplomacy multipliers," a beacon of hope for the democratic aspirations of oppressed peoples all over the globe.

Elite forces are truly "quiet professionals": their actions speak louder than words. They are self-motivated, self-confident, versatile, seasoned, mature individuals who rely on teamwork more than daring-do. Unfortunately, theirs is dangerous work. Since "Desert One"—the 1980 attempt to rescue hostages from the U.S. embassy in Tehran, for instance—American special operations forces have suffered casualties in real world operations at close to fifteen times the rate of U.S. conventional forces. By the very nature of the challenges which face special operations forces, training for these elite units has proven even more hazardous.

Thus it's with special pride that I join you in saluting the brave men and women who volunteer to serve in and support these magnificent units and who face such difficult challenges ahead.

Colonel John T. Carney, Jr., USAF-Ret.
President, Special Operations Warrior Foundation

There are two types of parachute jump: High Altitude High Opening (HAHO) and High Altitude Low Opening (HALO).

WORDS TO UNDERSTAND

lethal: Deadly.

aviation: Having to do with airplanes.

regimes: Rulers and their governments.

propaganda: Making many people believe in a particular view of events.

THE USAF AND PRISONERS

Pilots in combat, and in particular the pilots of the United States Air Force, almost always operate over enemy lines. This means that if they are shot down and survive, there is a big risk that they will become prisoners of war.

Ever since pilots took to the skies on combat missions, they have run the risk of becoming prisoners of war, otherwise known as POWs. During World War II, huge numbers of U.S. and Allied fighters and bombers were shot down over Germany, occupied Europe, and in Asian countries during the war against Japan. They were lucky to survive, but danger still faced them. Some were killed by angry crowds of people as soon as they landed in their parachutes. Some were forced to go into hiding and attempt long and dangerous journeys to escape the enemy. Yet others were captured, and they ended up as POWs.

In prison, the prison officers tried to get as much information out of them as possible. This process is called "interrogation." Sometimes, the interrogators tried to trick the pilot into releasing important and secret information about his battle plans. Other times, they actually tortured the man to get him to speak. The treatment depended very much on who was in charge in the prison and what sort of personalities the prison guards had.

This U.S. para is carrying the infamous Bazooka antitank rocket, which can fire a 60-mm rocket a distance of 1,948 feet (594 m).

In the history of the United States air forces, one of the worst places to become a prisoner was over North Vietnam during the Vietnam War. North Vietnam was a communist country attempting to take over South Vietnam. From 1965, U.S. aircraft started to bomb North Vietnam when it became involved in the war. On February 13, 1965, President Lyndon B. Johnson authorized Operation "Rolling Thunder"—one of the biggest bombing campaigns in history. Only nine months later, over a million tons of U.S. bombs had exploded inside North Vietnam—around 800 tons of bombs every single day. Rolling Thunder lasted for three years, and the U.S. Airforce (USAF), U.S. Navy, and U.S. Marine Corps aircraft flew more than 304,000 missions.

Bombing raids over North Vietnam during the Vietnam War were conducted by B52 Stratofortress aircraft. Working in groups of three, B52s could bomb a target area of three square miles (4.8 sq km).

The SA-2 Guideline, which was the main surface-to-air missile of the North Vietnamese in the fight against America during the Vietnam War.

The United States. had more airborne weaponry available to them than any nation on Earth. Aircraft such as the Phantom, Thunderchief, Skyhawk, and Skyraider flew right into the heart of enemy territory. There they dropped bombs and destroyed their targets, before attempting to fly back to the safety of South Vietnam. The power of this airborne armada was amazing. Yet North Vietnam did not intend to take this punishment lying down.

As Rolling Thunder intensified, the North Vietnamese started to build up more and more weaponry designed to shoot American aircraft down. In 1965, heavy machine guns were North Vietnam's main weapon. The danger of these to U.S. aircraft was very real. U.S. aircraft had to fly through storms of bullets, which took a heavy toll on aircraft and pilots—over 80 percent of the 3,000 American aircraft lost in the war were simply shot down by guns. By 1967 the situation was even worse. North Vietnam had acquired one of the most **lethal**

A pilot who is shot down will often activate a homing beacon. This emits a signal that gives a rescue helicopter a precise location.

U.S. Air Force soldiers with an AGM-65 Maverick ground-to-air missile during the Gulf War in 1991. The airplane is an A-10 Thunderbolt.

air defense systems anywhere in the world. It had purchased from Russia a terrifying new missile called the SA-2 Guideline. The Guideline was a type of missile known as a surface-to-air missile (SAM for short). Once it was fired, it flew to its target using radar. It could hit American aircraft at around 69,060 feet (18,000 meters). This meant that U.S. pilots had to fly through bullets at low levels and dodge Guidelines at high levels. In addition to the lethal North Vietnamese air defenses, the U.S. pilots also faced the North Vietnamese Air Force (NVAF). In 1967, North Vietnam had an air force of around 80 fighters, mainly MiG jet fighters. MiGs were maneuverable and powerful aircraft, which in the Vietnam War usually had the advantage of operating over their own territory with SAMs to help them win.

Because of all the weapons North Vietnam had at its disposal, many U.S. aircraft were shot down. Some 586 USAF pilots were captured or declared missing between 1962 and 1973. In 1967 alone, 297 American aircraft were destroyed on Rolling Thunder missions. If the pilot survived, both American and North Vietnamese soldiers would rush to try to get the pilot before the other. Massive effort went into rescuing U.S. pilots who had received years of expensive **aviation** training and possessed valuable information about U.S. aircraft. Yet sadly, the North Vietnamese often got

A monument to captured U.S. pilots in Hanoi, Vietnam. At the close of the Vietnam War, some 2,387 servicemen were also listed as missing.

there before the pilots' comrades, and they became prisoners of one of the cruelest **regimes** in history.

Captured American pilots were used by North Vietnam for **propaganda** and information. This actually saved them from being immediately killed. Instead, they were often paraded through the streets and filmed for North Vietnamese newsreels, then taken to one of a number of prisons in the city or district of Hanoi, the capital of North Vietnam. Among the worst of these was a prison called Hoa Lo Prison in the center of Hanoi, which the U.S. pilots nicknamed the "Hanoi Hilton." Many other prisons also became infamous.

 ## MAKE CONNECTIONS: EJECTION SEATS

When pilots in a modern jet are shot down, the best way to escape is by using their ejection seats. These are the seats in which they fly the aircraft. If they need to escape from the aircraft, they can do so by pulling a lever that detonates a small explosive charge under the seat. At the same time, the cockpit glass flies off and the pilots are blown clear of the aircraft, still in their seats. This is a painful experience—pilots will travel several hundred feet (many tens of meters) in less than a second—but at least they are alive. Once they are clear of the aircraft, their parachutes open, and they float back down to earth.

TEXT-DEPENDENT QUESTIONS

1. What is interrogation? What two forms might it take?
2. What was one of the worst places to be shot down and taken prisoner?
3. What was the SA-2 Guideline? Why was it so effective against American forces?
4. How many U.S. Air Force pilots were captured or declared missing during the Vietnam War?
5. What was the "Hanoi Hilton?"

In all these places, horrifying torture became a daily reality for the vast majority of captured airmen. The torture was inventive and cruel. It was often kept up for many days, even weeks. The aim was to break down the pilot's determination to withhold information so that he would tell military secrets to the North Vietnamese. The torture was so bad that many American pilots finally broke down and gave information. But this was usually only after many months, even years, of heroic resistance.

Because of the experience in Vietnam, all pilots in the USAF are now trained in the skills of surviving prison and interrogation, or evading capture in the first place. This program of training is known as SERE. SERE stands for Survival, Evasion, Resistance, Escape—the key elements a pilot needs if he

RESEARCH PROJECT

Look up more about the United States' SERE program. Where are soldiers trained for SERE? What does the SERE insignia look like? What does each part of the insignia mean? What are some of the things taught in the program? Does it include survival at sea?

or she is shot down behind enemy lines. Survival means staying alive and living off the land for weeks at a time, even when the availability of food and water is low. Evasion means avoiding the enemy, and moving only when it is safe. Resistance is training in standing up to interrogation and not giving away vital information. Finally, Escape means just what it says—escaping from captivity and finding your way to safety.

In this book, we will look at how American pilots train to cope with the worst that captivity can throw at them. We will learn from the experts how to keep mind and body healthy, and how to stay focused on never giving in to the enemy.

WORDS TO UNDERSTAND

human rights: The rights and freedoms you're entitled to simply because you're a human being. All humans deserve these rights.

resolve: A firm decision to a course of action.

fatigue: Tiredness.

contract: To get or catch an illness.

psychological: Having to do with the mind and the emotions.

BEING A PRISONER

Being captured by the enemy can be a terrifying experience. Your future seems entirely in the hands of your captors, and you do not know when you will see your loved ones again. Members of the U.S. Air Force are trained in the art of mental resilience so they can survive this harrowing experience.

One of the first things a U.S. pilot must do when training to survive captivity is find out what being a prisoner is really like. For an elite and highly trained pilot, courage and endurance are needed in major quantities if he or she is to survive a period in captivity. The enemy will understand how important their prisoner is. All their efforts will be to extract as much valuable information out of that person as possible.

Unfortunately, many governments around the world do not have a belief in **human rights.** This can mean that torture might be used to extract information if soldiers are unwilling to share their knowledge (and being elite soldiers, that is almost always the case). Thus a terrible battle begins—the captor using all the means at his disposal to forcibly pull information from captives' lips, and the captives relying on their training, but more important, on their strength of will and intelligence, to resist giving away vital facts. It is an immense test of resolve.

While being interrogated, this soldier is made to kneel in a stressful position. After a few hours, this will become incredibly painful.

Pilots who eject from their aircraft always carry a basic survival pack. This contains equipment such as waterproof matches, a small fishing kit, a survival blanket, a survival knife, and a compass.

Whatever the mental strength of the prisoners, the odds are stacked against them if they are in the hands of an intelligent interrogator. Many countries spend as much time and money investigating how to make people talk as others do in resisting interrogation. Furthermore, expert interrogators will usually know exactly what type of training the soldier has had for this situation. That means they know exactly how the person will resist.

But this is not the full picture. When we tend to think of the horrors of detention, we often focus on the experience of torture. Yet this is only one possible element of detention. It is also far from the most common. From the point of view of survival, everything about being a POW is usually designed to make the prisoner feel depressed, and leave the captive bored, lonely, uncomfortable, and confused. Once he or she is in this condition, it is easier for the captors to break the captive's will and make the captive talk.

A prisoner must calm his mind if he is to cope with the terrible boredom of captivity.

One of the biggest problems facing a captured pilot is loneliness and boredom. Pilots tend to be people who live exciting lives with lots of friends around them and plenty of activity. Captors often realize this, so they tend to place elite soldiers in places where they are isolated from people. The only people they see usually are the prison guards. The prison cell in which they are held is frequently very small. This means that the soldiers cannot move around as much as they would like. These conditions can start to break the pilots' will if they are not strong people and well trained. First, they may become less interested in looking after themselves. The outside world can start to seem less real. These feelings are what the captors want, because they enable them to draw out information from the prisoners. The reason for this is that the information does not feel as important to the pilots as it did when they were on the outside.

Another problem for pilot survivors is that if they are held long enough, they can begin to feel safe in the prison. This happens because

He can also relieve boredom by moving around.

they forget what it is like to live outside. This may seem strange, but remember that in the Vietnam War some pilots were kept on their own for two or three years without any contact with their friends or relatives. They did not even know what was happening in the news. The prison became their entire world.

In these situations, the only human contact the prisoners receive is that of the guards. This can actually mean that the prisoners look forward to the guards' visits—anything to break the hideous boredom. The guards will often pretend to be the prisoners' friends so they will trust them and start to talk. Trained pilots will recognize that this is what the captors are trying to do, however, and they will always watch what they say. Yet, the longer prisoners spend in detention, the further removed they may feel from their families and friends and the more depressed they can become. Thus, they will probably come to welcome any human contact, and the enemy interrogators may cleverly fill this gap with their own people.

In 1973, the North Vietnamese released 512 American prisoners of war (some of which are shown here) in "Operation Homecoming."

Of course, not all prisoners are kept alone. Some are kept in cells with one or two other people, while others are packed tightly into small rooms with lots of prisoners. This last situation can be as depressing as being by yourself. With little space, it is difficult to move around, the cell gets incredibly hot, and people can start to argue with each other because of the frustration. Again, this is something that the captors may be doing deliberately. If the people in the prison cell fall out with one another, they will not be as loyal to their comrades, and they might be more likely to talk.

Another problem associated with being held captive is that time goes incredibly slowly. Often the prisoner will not have anything to do at all—no books, no

MAKE CONNECTIONS: BURMA-THAILAND RAILWAY

During World War II, the Japanese army was famous for being cruel to its prisoners. A grim example from history is the Burma-Thailand railroad network, which was built by Allied POWs and native laborers. Prisoners were given almost no food and water, even though they had to work over 14 hours each day. They had to lay railroad lines in the blistering heat, while mosquitoes gave them malaria, an illness that can be life-threatening. The railroad was thousands of miles long, and many prisoners could not survive the tough regime. The type of work forced upon the prisoners resulted in the deaths of some 102,000 prisoners.

TEXT-DEPENDENT QUESTIONS

1. What is a POW? What does it stand for?
2. In what ways is the experience of being a POW designed to be negative?
3. Why might a POW experience loneliness? Why is this so hard?
4. How is it that the outside world can start to seem less real to a prisoner?
5. Why are prisoners so prone to getting sick?

games, no possessions, nothing. This will cause time to pass incredibly slowly. Boredom will cause physical discomfort as the mind makes the body fidget in an attempt to find anything to do. This, in turn, leads to a build-up of anxiety which over several months or years can crush the will to continue. It will even make you feel incredibly tired. Try sitting very still for a few hours without movement or entertainment. Your mind will start to feel very tired in spite of the fact that you are not physically working.

Not all prisoners are kept inside cells all day. Many POWs are made to work incredibly hard. This results in prisoners suffering from **fatigue**. Prisoners of war are often put to work as slave workers. Many prisons do work the prisoners hard. The hard work is made worse by a lack of proper food and rest. This can make the prisoners very weak and depressed. All prisoners should try to save as much energy as possible. That means resting when they are not working and trying to eat and drink as much as possible.

RESEARCH PROJECT

In 1964, Everett Alverez, a pilot in Vietnam, was the first American pilot shot down and taken captive during the Vietnam War. Look up more information about Alvarez. How long was he a prisoner? Where was he held? When he returned to the United States, what jobs did he do?

The combination of boredom, stress, overwork, and poor food means that prisons are very unhealthy places. Military prison camps tend to make prisoners weak and undernourished. In this condition, the prisoner will be prone to get ill. A poor diet results in a poor immune system—the parts of the body that fight off illnesses. The prisoners are much more likely to **contract** illnesses, and the illnesses tend to be more serious when they do. Illness is not only a physical problem. It also makes POWs very unhappy and pessimistic, and they can start to worry much more about making it out of prison.

These factors are just a few of the things that assault the mind and body of a pilot under the detention of the enemy. Such conditions are faced by almost all those captured by an enemy. But for elite soldiers, there is the added problem that they will attract interrogation. Elite soldiers are more likely than, say, an army cook, to attract the attention of the special interrogator. The interrogator's purpose is to use physical or **psychological** methods to make the captive talk. As we shall see in the next chapter, their "skills" and tools can be very powerful.

INTERROGATION

You have to be tough to survive interrogation. The secret is not to keep reminding yourself of what you must not say, but not doing anything that might make your interrogation worse. It is a difficult balance, but one that elite soldiers are trained to master.

One of the first methods used by the interrogator is the actual room in which the prisoner is kept. American pilots in Vietnam's infamous Hanoi Hilton found themselves in squalid and tiny cells. These were often almost pitch black. They generally had no toilet facilities and were full of rats, cockroaches, and huge spiders. The prisoner thus became dirty and had to constantly fight off the often aggressive insects and animals.

The cell is important to the interrogator as a place from which the prisoner will long to escape. The interrogator will make the prisoner aware that all he or she has to do is talk, and then they will be given a clean cell, a hot bath, and proper food. Over time, the interrogator hopes that the prisoner will give up vital information just for physical comfort.

The interrogator, however, may choose a different environment for the prisoner. Sometimes he will deliberately make a room that contains absolutely nothing to do and nothing interesting to see. This is usually a featureless cell without natural light (thus the prisoner loses track of time

A Korean soldier interrogates a Vietcong guerrilla. 47,000 Korean soldiers fought against the communists during the Vietnam War.

The "Hanoi Hilton," the horrifying destination for many U.S. airmen in Vietnam. Some walls of the prison had glass embedded in the top so that they were almost impossible to climb over without injury.

and date), without noise, and with nothing to entertain. Clothing is also selected to be very soft so as to create little sensation on the skin. Research has shown that this form of torture—called "sensory deprivation"—is actually one of the cruelest things of all. Prisoners in these conditions become very worried and crave human contact very badly.

Both the filthy cell and the sensory-deprivation cell help the interrogator to show that he has absolute power over the prisoner's life. He can then start to ask the prisoner direct questions. Sometimes he might use physical punishment—torture—to try to get the person to speak. Yet there is another method of interrogation that does not involve violence. This is called "brainwashing."

During brainwashing, the prisoner will meet a smart interrogator. The interrogator then teaches the soldier why it is wrong that the prisoner's country is fighting against the enemy's country. This may seem harmless, but the interrogator will keep the "lessons" going for weeks at a time. The soldier will be kept awake at nights while these lessons are going on so that he becomes less able to resist what the interrogator is saying. The interrogator hopes that eventually the soldier will give in and admit that his country is wrong. Once he has done this, the interrogator can get information out of the soldier. He can also use him for propaganda purposes, putting him in films and magazines criticizing his own country.

If brainwashing does not work, physical torture might be used. Torture comes in many different types, and it would not be pleasant to list them all here. However, what the torturer is trying to do is to break the soldier's will through physical pain. If the soldier does not talk, the pain is increased. If he does talk, the pain is lessened. It has to be said that most people will eventually break under physical torture over a long period. However, in Vietnam and other conflicts, some American pilots held out for many months. One or two never gave up any valuable information, despite years of abuse at the hands of their captors.

Sometimes, interrogators will use more **subtle** methods of getting information out of the prisoner. One of the most cunning of these is the use of a person who pretends to be a prisoner, but who is actually working for the enemy. This person will get into discussions with the other prisoners. Because the other prisoners think that the person is one of them, they might tell him some of the secrets they are holding. The "double agent" will be very hard to spot since they are specially trained to deceive the other prisoners.

There are no hard-and-fast rules for surviving an interrogation. However, USAF pilots and elite soldiers worldwide have rules about what to do and what not to do:

- Do not challenge your interrogators—this will only make them angry and may make them hurt you more during the interrogation.
- Focus on things that make you calm. For example, if you are being shouted at in a room with a window, focus your attention more on the warm sunlight outside than on the stream of abuse.
- During brainwashing, pretend that you are interested in what they are saying. This will make the enemy think they are making progress, and you will have time to save your physical energy. But be careful; the interrogators will be experts in spotting whether you are lying or not. Do not make things too easy for them.
- Keep reminding yourself there are people outside the prison who are

MAKE CONNECTIONS: READING LIES

A trained interrogator can often tell when someone is lying because of the things they do with their body and words. These include:

- Rubbing their nose or ear nervously while talking.

- The person keeps looking up while talking—this often means that the person is using their imagination to invent a story.

- The person's feet and hands are always shifting and twisting.

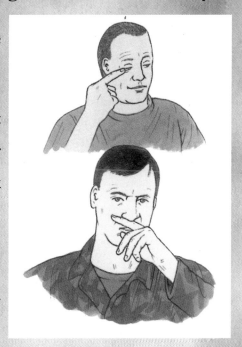

- The story does not come out easily. When people are telling the truth, they usually speak quickly and confidently.

- The person cannot look the interrogator in the eye, though this could be caused by fear.

working to get you released or win the war and free you. This will give you hope that the interrogation is not going to last forever.

- If you have to give information, hold on for a few days. Your comrades

TEXT-DEPENDENT QUESTIONS

1. Describe the cell where prisoners are held. Why is this important to the interrogation process?
2. Why are prisoners often denied natural light?
3. What is brainwashing? How does it help an interrogator get information from a prisoner?
4. What is a double agent? Why are they so hard to spot?
5. What are two rules to help someone survive an interrogation?

Nonviolent interrogation is often used as a way of befriending the prisoner in the hope that he offers to talk voluntarily.

RESEARCH PROJECT

Many action movies have scenes where the main character or an enemy is interrogated to get information out of them. Think of a movie you've watched recently that has such a scene. How is the scene similar to what you've read in this chapter? How is it different? Write a paragraph comparing and contrasting to the two scenarios. Then use the library or the Internet to read a first-hand account of someone who was interrogated. Now compare and contrast this account with both the movie scene and what is described in this book. What are the most important differences?

back at base will know that you have been captured, and they can change their plans in case you give anything away.

- If you are going into action in a group, make up a false story about your mission. If your group is captured, you can all come out with the same false story and possibly convince your enemy that you do not know anything important.

These steps can help a soldier survive interrogation, but it will still be tough. The most important thing is that the soldier still believes that he or she can hold out. The soldier who has the attitude "You cannot beat me," is most likely to survive mentally. So what do you need to do to survive the rest of prison life? This is the subject of the next chapter.

WORDS TO UNDERSTAND

self-discipline: The ability to control your actions, no
matter what you're feeling.

priority: Whatever is most important.

SURVIVING PRISON LIFE

Prison life varies tremendously from place to place. Sometimes prisoners are treated well, sometimes very badly. The USAF pilot is trained to survive, whatever the circumstances.

All elite soldiers go through SERE training. This is to help them survive capture by the enemy. SERE training is designed to be as realistic as possible. The instructors will dress up as enemy guards and speak in foreign languages. The "prisoners" will be shouted at, kept awake throughout the nights, and questioned all the time to try to get information.

This type of training can be very hard, but it is important. By being trained in this way, a soldier will know something of what might happen if he or she is captured. This means that the experience will not be as much of a shock, and the soldier can think clearly about how to survive.

However, training can only teach so much about surviving captivity. The most important thing is the soldiers' characters. If people give in whenever there are problems, or moan about their worries, then they are not likely to cope well with the experience of being held in captivity. Yet if they have **self-discipline**, with a good sense of humor and a strong desire to come through alive, they have a much better chance of surviving until they are released.

A POW training center in Reno, Nevada. Barbed wire and razor wire fences are difficult to escape across, especially if they are electrified.

In the Gulf War, U.S. troops captured their first Iraqi prisoners on January 19, 1991. They went on to capture thousands.

Though character cannot be taught, there are some principles of survival that can be learned. The most important are listed here.

Control what can be controlled

In prison, the temptation is to feel that you are completely helpless and at the mercy of the prison guards. You must overcome this feeling if you are to survive for long periods. The first thing to do is to set up as much of a routine as possible. This helps you keep track of the days and feel like you are still in control of your life. There are many things prisoners can do with their time. Perhaps they can hold discussion groups with fellow prisoners at certain times

Prison guards throw rubbish deliberately into the prisoner's cell because a dirty cell makes life even more unpleasant for him.

Or they could simply clean the corner of the cell. By doing simple things such as these, the soldiers will feel better about themselves and more in control. By feeling more in control, they are more likely to stay positive and believe that they will be rescued or escape.

Keep fit

Keeping fit in detention is not always easy, especially if you are held in cramped conditions and the food is poor. Fitness helps the mind to stay stronger, so the prisoner should try to keep up some form of exercise program. Work especially on the legs and arms, as you will need both to be strong if you are suddenly faced with the opportunity for a rescue attempt.

A U.S. pilot tends a garden in a Vietnamese prison. Such images were used by the North Vietnamese to suggest that they treated their prisoners well, but in reality they were regularly tortured.

If you are in very cramped conditions, simple stretching exercises and basic arm and leg strengthening exercises will stop muscles from wasting and help the mind stay healthier. However, there is one important point to remember: Prisoners should not exercise if they are very weak or ill. This is because it will burn up their energy, and they need all their energy to stay alive.

Keep the mind alert

Mental alertness is extremely difficult to maintain when you are isolated and bored. Try to develop mental projects for yourself—such as writing a book in your head (doing, say, a chapter each day). Basically, do anything to keep the brain active and sharp.

During the Vietnam War, some USAF prisoners set themselves amazing mental tasks to help them survive. One pilot built his dream home in his head. He did not just plan how his home would be built, but actually imagined it being built in the same time as it would take in reality. Working from the foundations to the roof, he "built" the home in just over a year. It was a long and exhausting project, but the important point was that it helped time to pass. If you are a prisoner, doing such mental tasks will also make you feel that your own personality and intelligence is not lost in the experience of captivity.

Do not make your enemy hate you

However much they dislike their captors, captured soldiers should never go out of their way to insult or challenge the enemy. The enemy does, after all, have control over how much food and water the prisoners receive, and what

MAKE CONNECTIONS: SAS TRAINING

The British SAS has one of the toughest training courses in the world for surviving prison and interrogation. At the end of SAS training—the final stage of which takes place in the jungles of Borneo—there is an Escape and Evasion exercise. If soldiers are caught, they are "interrogated" by their instructors for several days. It is vital that the soldiers do not give away any important information during the interrogation. If they do, they will not be allowed to join the SAS. Often the soldiers are kept blindfolded for several days, left in cold cells for hours, shouted at, and even left in the middle of fields while cars drive at speed around them. All this happens when they are exhausted anyway from a punishing march across the mountains, and only the toughest soldiers keep their mouths shut.

sort of treatment they get. If prisoners do something to make the captors unhappy, the prisoners' situation could get much worse. As a prisoner, your **priority** should be survival, not winning your own private war. That is why you should be as cunning as possible with your captors. Strike up conversations with ones who are in any way friendly. This will make them less willing to harm you, and it may even bring about better treatment.

During SAS escape training, the soldier must escape from soldiers, tracker dogs, and helicopters for a period of about 24 hours.

Also, it may make them give away information about the way that the prison works. This could help you escape.

Help each other

If pilots are in the company of other military prisoners, they should still respect the rank of other soldiers (though they should beware of giving away the rank of important officers to the captors). Being a prisoner should not be treated as a "time out" in military service. Instead, the soldiers should treat it as part of their operation and keep military discipline at all times. This also involves helping out their fellow prisoners. Being supportive of each other will make prison less lonely. A good group of comrades can help out when things get tough, and can also keep up a sense of humor, which can really help you survive mentally.

Plan to escape

Even if escape is almost impossible, it is still a good idea to plan such an attempt. This is not only because you may win your freedom. It also helps keep the mind alert and lively. Plan your escape as thoroughly as possible (see the

A Vietcong suspect is tied up and blindfolded during U.S. operations by the 25th Infantry Division in Vietnam.

next chapter) and keep on the lookout for any moments when it can be put into action. By having an escape plan in the back of your mind, you will also feel more in control of your destiny and less helpless before the prison guards.

Following these principles and mental activities can make a period in detention

RESEARCH PROJECT

This chapter recommends that prisoners stay in good physical shape, but this is not always easy when you're trapped in a tiny cell. What are some exercises or stretches that you can do without having a lot of space? Use the Internet to look up some ideas. Can you do any of these exercises at home to stay in shape?

survivable. A lot of these activities require good self-discipline to pursue. Again, this depends on your character. The main point is not to become dependent upon the prison environment, and to keep enough dignity to assure yourself that it is not where you belong.

TEXT-DEPENDENT QUESTIONS

1. Why is SERE training important?
2. Why should a prisoner try to set up a routine for his life?
3. Why is it important for a prisoner to stay physically fit?
4. What are some of the ways a prisoner can keep his mind sharp?
5. When more than one soldier is kept prisoner together, how should they treat each other?

WORDS TO UNDERSTAND

essential: Most important.

initial: Having to do with what came first.

ESCAPE

Escape is the most exciting thought for a prisoner. But an escape must be rigorously planned and executed if it is to succeed, which can be difficult if the prisoner is tired and hungry. Being recaptured is a very unpleasant prospect, because the prisoners' treatment at the hands of their captors is likely to be far worse than before they escaped.

There are no hard and fast rules about escaping from imprisonment. A successful escape plan depends on luck as much as planning. It has to be said that escape can be incredibly difficult from a maximum security military prison. Yet not all military prisons have high security. Because POWs are often captured in large numbers, many prisons are hastily built camps. The security on these may be open to an escape attempt. However, military prisons have lots of guards who are all heavily armed. Any attempt to escape will often result in death if you are seen. That is why you need a good escape plan.

When planning to escape, your mind should keep focused on the following points: Watch out for any routines in the prison that you can use to your advantage—times when there are fewer guards on duty, or times when vehicles make deliveries. Remember these patterns, and build up in your mind a profile

Barbed or razor wire is usually found at the perimeter of prison camps. Since it snags on clothing, it is very difficult to climb over.

Watchtowers usually feature one or two soldiers armed with rifles and controlling spotlights.

of how the prison operates. This should tell you when and where the security in the prison is at its weakest. This also involves using your senses. Keep eyes and ears open at all times to gather more and more information. Try to get friendly guards to reveal crucial information in-advertently. Also, try to get jobs within the prison that might put you in places from where it is easier to escape.

You must also have a plan. Escape can and does happen on the spur of the moment, but even if the occasion does occur, you should have planned in detail what your course of action will be. Planning helps the mind to stay in focus and helps you get ready for the escape event. Rehearse the escape in your mind time and time again, introducing various disasters to test whether your plan works or not. This basic mental preparation can help give you confidence during an actual escape attempt.

When the moment for escape comes, you must throw all your efforts into it. Your intention should be to get as far away from the prison as possible, to avoid being recaptured, and to get to safety. These are the skills of evasion.

Evasion is a skill taught to most troops. It applies not only to those who have escaped, but also to those who have yet to be caught. Surviving in the wild

Soldiers evading capture must cover as much ground as possible when it is safe to do so. During times of danger, they must lie low.

while trying to evade capture is an extremely difficult situation. The body will quickly become tired and dirty. This may lead to depression, and the escaped prisoner can then lose the will to continue. Fear may also prey on the mind, the fear of what will happen to you if you are captured or recaptured.

The way around these problems is to have a clear plan. The most **essential** points of evasion planning are:

- Have a clear idea of where you are going. Uncertainty can lead to despair, so soldiers must have some idea of what their objectives are. These should be broken down into hourly, daily, and weekly objectives so that time is tightly controlled.

- During the early stages of evasion, soldiers should try to put as much distance between themselves and the prison as possible. If only five miles

Soldiers must not leave signs of their presence when evading capture. This soldier is taking food from a field while lying on his belly so that he does not leave footprints in the mud at the edge of the field.

(8 km) are traveled from the starting point, then that will give a possible 78 square mile area (125 sq km) for the searchers to cover. The greater the distance from the prison, the more options the soldiers will have if they need to change their plan. Also, every mile walked can breed confidence in the soldiers and make them more certain that they are going to succeed.

- If you are evading capture, you should use your intelligence and training to avoid the pursuers. If you are moving through a civilian area, try to look as natural as possible; carrying a spade or similar civilian item can help you to blend in with others. Obviously, however, this depends on your having the ability to speak the language of the people around you. Do not try to communicate with them unless you have a perfect grasp of the language. Try to stay away from dogs. They are often the first to pick up on strangers.

- If you are in the countryside, you should occasionally walk in twisted,

Camouflaged uniforms were first introduced in the French-Indian War of 1754-63, when a company of Rangers wore green and brown uniforms to help them ambush the French soldiers.

MAKE CONNECTIONS: TRACKING SKILLS

Tracking skills can be very useful for escaping soldiers. They help them to know where the enemy is and whether they are about to walk into a trap. Signs that the enemy is in the area are:

- Moved stones, crumbled stones, or those pressed into the earth.
- Bushes or grasses bent down—these show that an enemy patrol has passed by the area.
- Stains—blood, water, and crushed leaves.
- Dropped litter.
- Footprints pressed into mud or soil.

TEXT-DEPENDENT QUESTIONS

1. What things should you be paying attention to when you're planning an escape?

2. Why is it important to plan your escape, instead of taking a spur-of-the moment opportunity?

3. What is evasion? Why is it such a difficult situation to be in?

4. Why is it important for soldiers to have a clear idea of where they are heading when they escape?

5. What are two ways to confuse tracker dogs that might be on your scent?

zigzagging patterns to throw off tracker dogs that are on your tail. If you do things like climb up and down trees, move across walls several times, and go in and out of streams, the tracker dogs will become confused and turn back on themselves.

• Make sure you get plenty to eat and drink on the journey and also that you let yourself sleep. Lack of food, drink, and sleep will make your mind confused. This, in turn, can lead to your making mistakes, which can then result in your being captured again. So sleep when necessary for short periods—even 20 minutes will help you to wake up with more energy and a clearer head. Steal food if possible to maintain your energy, but be aware not to leave any tracks or be detected. When stealing crops, a good

RESEARCH PROJECT

This chapter suggests short, twenty-minute naps to help you regain your energy quickly. Recent studies have shown that short naps, or power naps, are a great way to help you get energy in your life, too! Use the Internet to find out more about power naps. Why is twenty minutes a good length of time to sleep? Do you dream during a nap like this? Why does taking a short nap make you feel more awake, even though you didn't get much sleep?

method is to lie over the edge of the field so you do not leave footprints in the soil.

- Make sure that you never drop any litter. The enemy can use this material to track you.

By looking after the body as much as possible and by having a plan, the chances are that this, combined with a lot of luck, will mean that an escape attempt succeeds. Of course, this assumes that soldiers have a generally firm will. Regardless of training, soldiers attempting to escape must apply themselves with strength and learn to tolerate discomfort, pain, and fear along the way. Thankfully for elite USAF pilots, their initial training period should have provided these skills anyway.

WORDS TO UNDERSTAND

improvise: Make something using whatever is handy.

hallucinate: See things that aren't really there.

SURVIVE IN THE WILDERNESS

Evasion is only one part of a successful escape attempt. Once soldiers escape, they must face the prospect of surviving in often hostile conditions with only the materials they have brought with them. Sometimes that may be nothing. Elite soldiers must learn to improvise if they are to survive.

The final element of this book is that of survival. Being in the wilderness without food, shelter, or water probably presents a bigger danger to life and health than the pursuers. The actual techniques of survival are not our focus here. Rather, what should be understood is how the environment affects the way your mind works and the will to survive.

We have already looked at the need for rest, food, and water. Shelter is just as important as these three. This applies even in warm countries, because the two biggest enemies of anyone exposed are cold and heat. Enduring extreme cold and extreme heat can lead to illnesses known as hypothermia and hyperthermia. Hypothermia (also called exposure) happens in situations of extreme cold. It is caused when the temperature in the middle of the human body falls below its safe level of 97.8-100.4°F (36-38°C). Hyperthermia (also called heatstroke) is the opposite—in very hot climates, the human body gets too warm, and the blood gets too thick to be pumped easily around the body by the heart.

A soldier dries out his feet while surviving in woodland. Leaving feet wet can literally make them rot, a condition called "trench foot."

Endurance is vital to survival, so training is hard. When a soldier is constantly running and moving, he can burn up 4,000 calories a day.

Both of these illnesses can kill if they are not treated immediately. A person with hypothermia needs to be warmed up, whereas a person with hyperthermia needs to be cooled down. Even the early stages of these illnesses are a problem for the escaping prisoner, because they affect the ability to think and make clear decisions. A person with either problem will become disorientated, confused, depressed, and may even start to **hallucinate**. For escaping prisoners, this means they are likely to make mistakes that could lead them to be captured again.

To protect themselves from cold weather, soldiers must follow several rules:

- Keep the head and hands covered up at all times.

MAKE CONNECTIONS: SKIN HEATING TECHNIQUE

The efficiency of this is best tested on your hands. If they are particularly cold, first touch them against a warm part of your body to remember their original temperature; then practice the following technique:

1) First imagine that hot blood is pumping right through the hands and into the fingertips.

2) While doing this, also imagine that you are immersing your hands in a thick, very warm, orange liquid.

3) As you do this, actually look at your hands and believe that you have total control over their temperature.

- Find a shelter, particularly at night. Old farm buildings can be good because they may have lots of hay and straw to make a warm bed. But make sure that you are not discovered there by a farmer or farm dog.

- Make sure you do not even begin an escape attempt if you do not have some form of appropriate clothing. There is no point in escaping only to die of exposure.

When evading the enemy, soldiers must avoid unnecessary exposure to the elements and dehydration, all of which increase tiredness.

RESEARCH PROJECT

Hyperthermia is not only a problem for people trying to survive in the wilderness. Long, hot summers can be dangerous, especially for those without air conditioning in their homes. Look up more information about heatstroke and heat exhaustion. What is the difference between these two conditions? Which is worse? Who is most likely to suffer from heatstroke? What are the best ways to prevent it?

- Try to stay as dry as possible.
- Keep out of very cold winds which can take all the body warmth.

Extreme heat can be just as serious as extreme cold. The soldier will become tired and apathetic, and must follow common-sense precautions like staying out of the sun, and drinking as much as possible. Shelter is vital, especially in the desert regions (one SAS soldier walked 160 miles (255 km) through desert during the Gulf War while fleeing Iraqi soldiers). Find caves to shelter in or make shelters out of pieces of material. If you have some water, do not drink it all at once. Ration it out slowly. Do not eat if there is not much water.

From a mental point of view, both heat and cold present the survival problem of fear. The escaping soldier will start to think about "freezing to death" or "dying of thirst." Believe it or not, just thinking about dying can make it more likely. Studies into people who have survived extreme survival situations usually showed that they never let go of the belief that they would survive. A strong

TEXT-DEPENDENT QUESTIONS

1. Why are both hot and cold weather dangerous when surviving in the wilderness?

2. What are three rules for protecting yourself from cold weather?

3. When trying to survive in hot weather, should you eat more or less food if you don't have much water?

4. Why is it dangerous for someone in the wilderness to think about dying?

mind seems to make the body stronger. Elite pilots and soldiers tend to have strong minds already from the hard training they have experienced. This gives them a good advantage when surviving an escape attempt.

In any survival situation, whether it is in a prison camp or on the run, having clear goals and a strong desire to survive are possibly the most important tools the soldier has in order to come out of the situation alive. Training does impart essential skills of survival, but the lesson seems to be that character can decide whether someone lives or dies in a survival or prison situation.

SERIES GLOSSARY OF KEY TERMS

camouflage: Something that makes it hard to distinguish someone or something from the terrain or landscape around them.

casualty: A person who is killed or injured in a war or accident.

covert: Done in secret.

dehydrated: When you don't have enough water in your body for it to function properly. Alternatively, dehydrated food is food that has had all the water removed so that it won't go bad.

dislocation: When a joint is separated; when a bone comes out of its socket.

edible: Able to be eaten.

exposure: A health condition that results from bad weather around you. For example, when you get hypothermia or frostbite from cold weather, these are the results of exposure.

flares: A device that burns brightly, and can be used to signal for help. They can only be used once.

hygiene: The techniques and practices involved with keeping yourself clean and healthy.

improvised: Used whatever was available to make or create something. When you don't have professionally made equipment, you can make improvised equipment from the materials naturally found around you.

insulation: Something that keeps you warm and protects you from the cold.

kit: All of the clothing and equipment carried by a soldier.

layering: A technique of dressing for the wilderness that involves wearing many layers of clothing. If you become too warm or too cold, it is easy to remove or add a layer.

marine: Having to do with the ocean.

morale: Confidence, enthusiasm, and discipline at any given time. When morale is high, you are emotionally prepared to do something difficult. When morale is low, you might be angry, scared, or anxious.

purification: The process of making water clean and safe enough to drink.

terrain: The physical features of a stretch of land. Hard or rough terrain might be mountains or thick forests, and easy terrain would be an open field.

windbreak: Something that you use to block the wind from hitting you. If you camp somewhere exposed to the wind, it will be very difficult to stay warm.

EQUIPMENT REQUIREMENTS

Compass
Flint and steel firelighter
Windproof matches
Striker board (for the matches)
Candle (some versions are edible)
Magnifying glass
Flexible saw
Lock knife/Swiss Army knife
Sewing thread
Needles
Single-edged razor
Heliograph (a mirror for signaling)
Fishing gear

Wire snare
Whistle
Water bag
Water purification tablets
Bag closures
Wound closures
Antiseptic
Adhesive bandages
Sunblock/insect repellent
Safety pin
Pencil
Notepad
Signal flares

USEFUL WEBSITES

If you want to find out more about a career in the USAF, go to the website: www.airforce.com. It will give you all the information you need about USAF jobs, and directions to your nearest recruiting office.

Other useful websites include:

www.USAF2000.com

www.airforcehistory.com

www.af.mil

www.pdas.com

FURTHER READING

Hearn, Chester G. *Air Force: An Illustrated History*. Minneapolis, Minn.: Compendium Publishing, 2008.

McCarthy, James. *The Air Force*. Andrews AFB, M.D.: Air Force Historical Foundation, 2002.

McManners, Hugh. *The Complete Wilderness Training Manual*. New York: DK Publishing, 2007.

Ross, Sue. *The Air Force Academy Candidate Book: How to Prepare, How to Get In, How to Survive Fifth Edition*. Monument, Co.: Silver Horn Books, 2012.

Wiest, Andrew. *The Vietnam War*. New York: Rosen Publishing Group, 2008.

ABOUT THE AUTHOR

Dr. Chris McNab has written and edited numerous books on military history and elite forces survival. His publications to date include *German Paratroopers of World War II, The Illustrated History of the Vietnam War, First Aid Survival Manual,* and *Special Forces Endurance Techniques*, as well as many articles and features in other works. Forthcoming publications include books on the SAS, while Chris's wider research interests lie in literature and ancient history. Chris lives in South Wales, U.K.

INDEX